Super Bouncy Ball

Kitchen Experiment

By Meg Gaertner

Published by The Child's World®
1980 Lookout Drive • Mankato, MN 56003-1705
800-599-READ • www.childsworld.com

Photographs ©: Rick Orndorf, cover, 1, 14, 16, 17, 18, 19, 20,
21; Steve Debenport/iStockphoto, 5; Shutterstock Images, 6,
10; Dmitry Naumov/Shutterstock Images, 7; Sheila Fitzgerald/
Shutterstock Images, 9; Africa Studio/Shutterstock Images, 13

ISBN 9781503825406
LCCN 2017959701

Printed in the United States of America
PA02378

Table of Contents

CHAPTER 1

Playing with Polymers

Everything is made of **atoms**. Atoms are tiny things that make up everything we see. They come together in groups called **molecules**. Molecules can have atoms all of one kind. They can also be made of many kinds of atoms.

Sometimes many molecules come together. They can form a **polymer**. All of the molecules in a polymer look the same. They line up in rows. Rows of polymers form solids.

Molecules are too small to see. But we can use models to look at their shapes.

Solids have their own shape. This shape stays the same. Chairs and rubber balls are solids.

Some polymers are found in nature. Hair and fingernails are polymers. Some polymers are made by people. Anything **plastic** is a polymer.

Hair are polymers. We can cut hair to make the polymers shorter.

Plastic is used to make toys, water bottles, and many other things.

You can use polymers to make a super bouncy ball at home. It will bounce high.

Plastic water bottles are polymers. We can recycle them to help the earth.

You will mix glue and a powder called borax. Glue is not a solid. But borax makes the molecules in glue stick together. The new polymer holds its shape. It forms a solid ball.

CHAPTER 2

Elasticity

Everything we see has **properties**. Properties are features that an object has. Size and shape are properties. We can measure an object's properties.

Chemical properties are measured by changing the atoms of an object. One way to do this is through a **reaction**. In a reaction, the atoms in an object change places. They can even mix with atoms from another object.

TIP

You can use a reaction to make pennies bright again. Mix water, vinegar, and salt. Add the pennies. The green color will disappear. The pennies will look like new!

Pennies all start out the same color. But they change over time.

Have you ever seen a green penny? Pennies are made of a metal called copper. New pennies are bright and reddish-brown.

A soccer ball is round. That is one of its physical properties.

But copper atoms join with molecules in the air. The pennies become less bright over time. They can even turn green or black.

Copper reacts with the air we breathe. This is a chemical property of copper.

Physical properties are measured without changing the atoms of an object. We can easily measure something's physical properties. Color and shape are physical properties.

Elasticity is another physical property. Elasticity measures how easily something can return to its first shape. Objects with elasticity can be bent and pulled. They can be stretched to become taller or longer.

TIP
Find a rock outside. What color is it? How big is it? You just noticed some of the rock's physical properties!

Have you ever stretched bubblegum between your fingers? Bubblegum stretches because it has high elasticity. It is elastic. It returns to its first shape after being stretched.

Something that is not elastic does not return to its first shape. It has low elasticity. Paper is not elastic. If you rip a piece of paper in half, it becomes two separate pieces. The paper does not go back together. It keeps its new shape.

Your super bouncy ball will be elastic. When the ball hits the ground, it becomes flat on one side. But elasticity helps the ball become round again. It also pushes the ball back up into the air. An elastic ball will bounce.

Bubblegum is elastic. You can blow big bubbles before it pops!

13

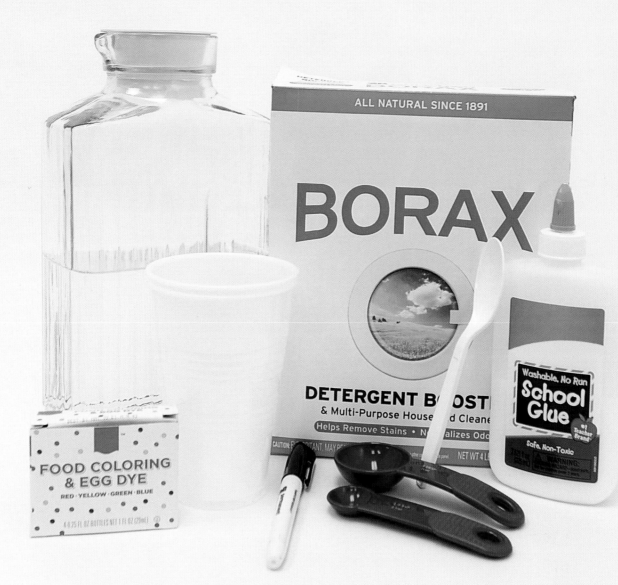

CHAPTER 3

THE EXPERIMENT
Let's Make a Bouncy Ball!

TIME TO FINISH: 5-10 minutes

5
10

MATERIALS LIST

marker
2 plastic cups
2 tablespoons (30 mL) warm tap water
1 teaspoon (2.5 mL) borax
spoon
food coloring
1 tablespoon (15 mL) glue

1. Use the marker to write a "1" on one of the cups. Write a "2" on the other cup.

2. Mix the warm water and borax in cup 1. Mix until you cannot see the borax.

TIP
Do not eat any of these supplies. They won't taste very good. They will make you feel sick.

3. Put the glue in cup 2. Add a few drops of food coloring. Mix well.

4. Add ½ teaspoon (2.46 mL) of the #1 mix to cup 2. But do not stir it yet!

5. Wait for 10–15 seconds. Then stir it all together.

6. When the glue becomes too hard to stir, use the spoon to take it out of cup 2. Shape the ball with your hands.

7. Keep rolling the ball between your hands. It will get less sticky.

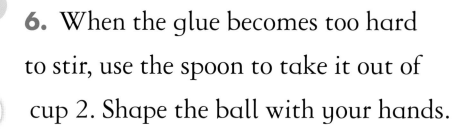

TIP

If the ball stays sticky, dip it into cup 1. Then roll it in your hands until it is dry.

8. Hold the ball 1 foot (30.5 cm) off a table. Drop the ball. It will bounce off the table!

TIP
You can measure how high your ball bounces. Hold a ruler in one hand. Drop the ball onto a table. How high did your ball bounce? How else might you measure your ball?

Glossary

atoms (AT-uhms) Atoms are little pieces that make up everything. Atoms come together to make molecules.

chemical (KEM-uh-kul) Something that is chemical must be changed to be seen or touched. A chemical property of pennies is that they change color over time.

elasticity (i-lass-TISS-uh-tee) Elasticity measures how easy it is for something to return to its first shape. Something that bounces has high elasticity.

molecules (MOL-uh-kyools) Molecules are groups of atoms. Sometimes molecules join to form polymers.

physical (FIZ-uh-kuhl) Something that is physical can be seen or touched. A physical property of a ball is that it is round.

plastic (PLASS-tik) Plastic is a type of man-made polymer. Water bottles are made from plastic.

polymer (POL-ih-mur) A polymer is a group of molecules that line up in a row. All of the molecules in a polymer look the same.

properties (PROP-ur-tees) Properties are features of objects. Properties can be seen or measured.

reaction (re-AK-shuhn) In a reaction, atoms in objects mix and change places. Pennies change color because of a reaction.

To Learn More

In the Library

Macken, JoAnn Early. *Plastic*. South Egremont, MA:
Red Chair Press, 2016.

Owen, Ruth. *Let's Investigate Everyday Materials*. New York, NY:
Ruby Tuesday, 2017.

Vogel, Julia. *Measuring Length*. Mankato, MN:
The Child's World, 2013.

On the Web

Visit our Web site for links about bouncy balls:
childsworld.com/links

Note to Parents, Teachers, and Librarians: We routinely verify our Web links to make
sure they are safe and active sites. So encourage your readers to check them out!

Index

About the Author

Meg Gaertner is a children's book author and editor who lives in Minnesota. When not writing, she enjoys dancing and spending time outdoors.